Africa
in Early Days

VOYAGES IN READING

General Editor:
Dr. Jack Cohn

OTHER TITLES IN THIS SERIES:

Jack London and Walt Whitman
O. Henry and Edgar Allan Poe

Africa
in Early Days

Sylvia C. Finkley

GENERAL EDITOR: *Dr. Jack Cohn*

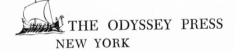 THE ODYSSEY PRESS
NEW YORK

PREFACE

This book is one in a new series of texts for students and general readers. Students in secondary schools, junior high schools, and intermediate or middle schools should find these books of particular interest.

The titles in this series have been selected with care and written or edited by knowledgeable teachers. This volume presents an introduction to the history and cultures of Africa before the Portuguese.

The vocabulary, though occasionally simple, includes a substantial store of more difficult words. A short glossary at the end of each book should make for quick discovery of definitions of words. However, not all difficult words have been defined in the glossary so that use of the dictionary may be encouraged.

These books may be used as classroom or supplementary texts, for individual instruction, in a variety of special programs, and for library or recreational purposes.

Dr. Jack Cohn

Contents

CHAPTER 1

The African Giant   1

An Unknown Land 1
Egypt and Ethiopia 4
Africa Below the Sahara 13

CHAPTER 2

Interesting Peoples of Africa   21

The Bushmen 24
The Bantus 28
The Hottentots 30
The Pygmies 32

CHAPTER 3

Life Among the Peoples of Africa   37

The Farmers and Cattlemen 37
The Builders 43
The Metal Workers 47
The Traders 50

CONTENTS

CHAPTER 4

Social Living   53

The Family   53
Love and Marriage   58
Religion and Morals   59
Education   65
Literature   67
Art   68

CHAPTER 5

Some Great Men in Africa's Past   71

Gunga Musa   71
Sonni Ali   72
Askia Muhammed   74

CHAPTER 6

Contact with Asia and Europe   77

The Mohammedans   77
The Portuguese   80

Glossary   83
Bibliography   85

Africa
in Early Days

CHAPTER 1

The African Giant

An Unknown Land

Africa has an ancient and honorable history. The sight or sound of the word "Africa" usually brings to mind vast jungles, wild beasts, and primitive people. An air of mystery has always hung over Africa. It has been called "the Dark Continent." It was not called "dark" because the sun does not shine there or because the people of the continent are yellow, brown, and black. It was called "dark" because little was known about this great land mass.

Africa is the continent where the human race began. There civilization reached very great heights in prehistoric times. By "prehistoric" we mean the age before records were kept. However, recently men have been very curious about "the Dark Continent."

Scientists have found fossil remains of prehistoric creatures and remains of ancient man, the first true man on earth. Here was a man who walked like a man. And he lived about a million years ago in southeastern Africa! Greek and Roman writers had recorded some facts about the great civilizations of Africa. Scientists have found ancient bones, ruins, and other relics of the past. These men have given us much information about the early African states and their way of life.

Africa is a vast continent. It could contain the United States three times over, with some land to spare. North Africa has a warm climate. Many people of different races came to this section of Africa because of the climate and the abundance of food.

To the south, the Sahara Desert reaches from the Atlantic Ocean to the Red Sea. There are many deserts in different parts of the world, but the Sahara is the largest, the hottest, and the driest. In very early times men could cross this desert only by camel. The desert seemed to separate the light-skinned Africans of the North from their darker-skinned brothers of the South.

With the exception of North Africa, the continent was difficult to reach. There were few harbors along the coast line. There were vast jungles inland, and the climate was extremely hot. Outsiders fell prey to disease. There were rivers on which boats could not sail. Travel in these areas was both difficult and dangerous.

The earliest time of which we have knowledge is the age of the River-drift man. These people lived in caves along the rivers. They ate berries, roots, fish, and small game. They did not cook their food for they had not discovered fire.

Then came the Rough Stone Age. The people of this age lived in cliffs above the water. Their weapons were made of stone and were very crude and rough. There followed a period of smooth, polished weapons, the Smooth Stone Age. Food was now cooked, as man had discovered fire. Animals were domesticated; the dog was the first animal to be tamed. When history began to be written, dogs, cows, sheep, goats, donkeys, and pigs were domestic animals. Man had used some of these animals to help him with his work. The men of this period learned how to sow grain and gather it. They made bowls and utensils of clay.

The discovery of metal and bronze took man into the Metal Bronze Age. Now sharper tools and weapons were made. These tools meant an improved way of living. Better weapons meant easier invasions and conquests. A tree could be cut down with a

3

bronze ax. Men began to live together. They formed villages and had permanent homes.

Egypt and Ethiopia

Some people believe that the life of the very first man began in Ethiopia. The Egyptians, though, believe that their country is the oldest in the world. In prehistoric days, many groups migrated to Egypt. People came from the eastern Mediterranean, Semitic peoples came from the East, and black and brown tribes came from the South. It has been said that a prince and his wife brought the beginning of civilization from Ethiopia to Egypt. From the mixing of all these groups came the native Egyptians.

During the Stone Age, the Egyptians were an agricultural people. They grew crops and developed a system of irrigation. They tamed animals which could help them in their work. As tools improved, they engaged in mining, brick-making, carpentry, weaving, and ship-building. The workers made many articles of use and beauty.

The Egyptians were builders. They built great palaces and pyramids. In order to do these things they had to have knowledge of physics, geometry, and engineering. The Ethiopians claim that they taught the primitive Egyptians to practice writing.

4

However, we do know that the Egyptians developed a means of expressing their thoughts in writing. The pictures that decorated their tombs and temples were used to tell a story. These pictures are called "hieroglyphics." A simple form of these pictures was developed for everyday use. Main outlines of the pictures were used to represent a word or an idea. This is known as hieratic writing. Late in the history of Egypt these hieratics were abbreviated. Dots and lines were substituted for more complex pictures. This system is known as demotic or common writing. The term "demotic" applies to the alphabet used by the ancient Egyptians. This was adopted by the people and can be compared to our modern shorthand.

Egyptian civilization began on the Nile River. In Africa, the land of surprises, the Nile River flows north through the desert. People usually settled near rivers. There the soil was rich, and crops could be grown. People had enough food to satisfy their needs.

The very heavy rains came each year in the early summer. The water in the Nile rose to flood level. Then water would flow over its banks onto the fertile Ethiopian land. The river carried this rich soil into Egypt. Every summer hundreds of miles of land were flooded. Then the water flowed back so that

it was again confined between its banks. The rich,
fertile soil that had been washed ashore was left.
Farmers sowed their seeds and their crops grew.
The Egyptians had more than enough food. Sometimes the floods were so great that even the Egyptian farm lands were flooded. Then again, there
might not be enough water to raise crops. Dikes,
dams, irrigation canals, and reservoirs were built to
store the water. These helped the people to raise their
crops when water was scarce. The Egyptians were
becoming engineers. They found the connection
between the time of the floods and the positions of
the stars. Thus began the study of astronomy. They
knew enough about the stars to make the first calen-
dar. They divided the year into 365 days. There
were twelve months of 30 days plus 5 extra days.

Two kingdoms grew out of the Egyptian city-
states. They were known as the kingdom of Upper
Egypt and the kingdom of Lower Egypt.

About 3300 B.C. the two kingdoms were united.
Memphis, near the present-day city of Cairo, became the capital. Menes wore the double crown;
the white crown of the south was joined with the
red crown of the north. Menes was the first king
of the Egyptians and the First Dynasty began with

6

him. These dynasties consisted of a series of rulers who belonged to the same family. The rulers were called "pharaohs."

From 3200 to 2780 B.C., the First and Second Dynasties ruled Egypt. The Third Dynasty came into being when a different family ascended the throne. This was the period of the Old Kingdom. The Old Kingdom included four dynasties, the Third through the Sixth. During this period the first pyramids were built. The most famous of these pyramids, at Gizeh near Cairo, is one of the wonders of the world. It has been said that these are the greatest tombs in human history.

Today, great dams are being built along the Nile. Water will eventually cover the places where the pyramids are located. Some pyramids are being moved—stone by stone—to preserve them.

The pharaohs who ruled from the Seventh through the Tenth Dynasties did so in disorder and quarreling. These were weak pharaohs, and there were several rival pharaohs ruling at the same time. In the south, the rich noblemen were scornful of these weak pharaohs. In 2100 B.C. the nobleman Intef made known publicly that he was the pharaoh. He named Thebes the new capital. He called himself the first king of the Eleventh Dynasty. Thus began a new period called "The Middle Kingdom." It was at this time that Egypt was again united under one ruler.

The next three dynasties were torn by civil wars. For more than a hundred years war raged. Thebes was the capital during the Thirteenth Dynasty. Memphis was the capital during the Fourteenth Dynasty. During this civil war, while the Egyptians fought each other, the Hyksos came in from the south. The Hyksos were a mixture of half-civilized peoples. They conquered Egypt, and the rulers called themselves pharaohs. They held Egypt during three dynasties. Sekenenre, an Egyptian nobleman, finally drove the Hyksos out of Thebes.

The Eighteenth Dynasty began in 1555 B.C. This dynasty marked the beginning of the New Kingdom. Nefertari was the famous Queen of Aahmes, King of Egypt. It was he who finally drove the Hyksos out and founded the Eighteenth Dynasty. Nefertari was a black woman of great beauty, strong personality, and a remarkable ability to rule. She was, for years, connected with the government of Amenhotep I, who succeeded his father. Queen Nefertari was greatly respected. Many monuments were raised in her honor. She was loved as the co-founder of the Eighteenth Dynasty.

The Eighteenth Dynasty flourished under the

8

pharaohs called Thothmes and Amenophis. Thothmes I was ruler of an Egypt which was the greatest empire the world had ever seen. He left his empire to his daughter Hatshepsut, aged twenty-four, and his seventeen-year-old son. Hatshepsut had her father's ability and energy. The son was weak and aimless. He died young and Queen Hatshepsut ruled for many years.

A woman on the throne of the pharaohs was an extraordinary thing for Egypt. The Egyptians made up for this by saying that Hatshepsut had received some special favor at birth. In some of the pictures in the temples, she was shown as a boy.

Egypt prospered under the rule of Queen Hatshepsut. Instead of building pyramids or tombs, she began to build a temple in which she might be worshipped after death. The approach to the temple was guarded on either side by a row of sphinxes. Queen Hatshepsut also built two obelisks of polished granite. Long explorations by sea along the east coast of Africa were made during her reign. One of these sea voyages was reputed to be 5,000 miles long. Pictures showing her trip to East Africa were found on the temple walls.

Thothmes III, a younger brother, grew restless at being held so long from the throne by his ambitious sister. The sudden death of the queen cast some doubt on the cause of her death. Thothmes III ordered that her name be removed from all the monuments she had built. He had his own name put in her place. The workmen did such a poor job that in many cases it has been possible to read the original name.

Amenophis V, a later ruler, took no interest in his empire. He went into the desert to live and his empire began to fall apart. Tut-ankh-Amen followed him as ruler. Although he lived to be only eighteen years old, his name is familiar to many. Rich remains of his kingdom were dug up recently by an Englishman named Howard Carter.

The greatest of the pharaohs of the Nineteenth Dynasty was Ramses II. He ruled for sixty-six years. During his reign, many great temples and pyramids were built. Ramses III ruled for twenty-one years. He was the last great pharaoh of Egypt. The end of the Twentieth Dynasty in 1090 B.C. saw the kingdom losing strength and power.

Four dynasties ruled during the Third Intermediate Period, from 1090 to 712 B.C. Some of the pharaohs were strangers from Ethiopia, Libya, and Nubia. The Ethiopians were the first people to smelt iron. As a result they made superior weapons and were able to conquer the Egyptians. They ruled Egypt for one hundred years. During this period a magnificent chapel was built at Karnak. The temple of Thebes was restored. But the Ethiopian pharaohs had difficulty controlling the Egyptians.

The Twenty-fifth Dynasty began what is called The Late Egyptian Period. It was marked by the Assyrian conquest of Egypt. They robbed and burned the City of Thebes. But the Assyrians too could not hold Egypt. They were forced to leave, and the Twenty-sixth Dynasty ruled in North Egypt.

In succeeding centuries Egypt was overrun by the Persians. Then Ptolemy, one of the generals of Alexander the Great of Macedon, ruled. The Greeks came, followed by the Romans. The fall of Rome brought in the Turks. Egypt was under the rule of the Sultans of Turkey for hundreds of years. During this long span of time, all of its former greatness was forgotten.

Ancient Ethiopia was south of Egypt. It included the present-day Ethiopia and the area known as Nubia. Today, most of the Ethiopians are descended from the Hamites. The rest are a mixture of several tribal groups—Somali, Shankalla, and others.

There was a flow of black people from the south into Egypt. The pharaohs could not keep the people of the Nubian desert from their land. A black man named Ra Malesi became pharaoh. After the eighteenth century B.C., Blacks became a part of the

11

Egyptian government. During the Hyksos invasion, many Egyptians ran away to the Upper Nile Valley. There they mixed freely with the black people.

It was a thousand years later that Piankhi, an Ethiopian, conquered Egypt. His brother, Shabaka, became the pharaoh in 710 B.C. He kept the peace as well as driving away the Assyrians. Other Ethiopian pharaohs found it more difficult to keep the Assyrians from invading their land. By 670 B.C. the Ethiopians had been driven out of lower Egypt.

When the Assyrians conquered Egypt, the Ethiopian rulers went back to their own country. There they ruled for many centuries. Their culture reflected the long contact they had had with Egypt. They built pyramids, temples, and baths at Napata and other Ethiopian cities. They also worshipped Egyptian gods.

Frumentius, a Syrian missionary, converted the Ethiopians to Christianity in 330 A.D. By the fourth century A.D., Ethiopia was a Christian dependency of the Roman Empire. For the next 1300 years, it controlled most of the Red Sea coast.

Christian Ethiopia stood firm against the war-like Mohammedans. After two centuries of struggle, it finally agreed to pay tribute to the Arabs.

The coming of the Greeks, then the Romans, and later, the Arabs, led the Ethiopians to make changes in their own culture. Much of what was native to this country has been lost.

Africa Below the Sahara

GHANA

Before the days of the great explorers, very little was known about Africa below the Sahara. This part of Africa, because of its swamps, great forests, and wild animals, was difficult to explore. When the Mohammedans went into West Africa in the seventh century, they found a civilization that was already more than a thousand years old.

We do know that between the years 300 and 1100 A.D., there was a powerful West African state known as Kumbi or Ghana. The people were peaceful. They engaged in farming and trading. Their capital, Kumbi-Kumbi, was a great trading center. The Mohammedans entered this empire in 1000 A.D. They were able to force their religion on some of the people, and many Mohammedans settled there.

Under the leaders of the Sisse ruling family, Ghana reached its height of power. Tribes to the north and south paid tribute to the king. During the eleventh century, Tenkamenin was King of Ghana. He ruled over a large empire. He was very rich and lived in a beautiful palace decorated with pictures and sculpture. An ancient writer said in 1067 that Tenkamenin held court with great pomp and ceremony. When he gave interviews, Tenkamenin appeared under a large tent which had a raised floor that rested on posts. Ten horses covered with gold cloth were lined up around this tent. Behind Tenkamenin stood ten servant boys carrying shields and swords decorated with gold. To the right of the king stood the sons of the princes of the empire, richly dressed. The governor of the town and all the ministers of the empire sat on the ground in front of the ruler. This was ancient Ghana at its height.

But Ghana began to decline at the end of the eleventh century. The climate had begun to change. The rivers dried up and became small streams, so that the soil was no longer rich. The Sahara Desert began to creep into the empire. Ghana no longer continued to be a prosperous country.

In 1076, the Almoravids or Mohammedans invaded the country. They took the capital and killed all those who would not accept their religion. Again the country was invaded, twice in the thirteenth century. Ghana, weakened by religious quarreling and by nature, fell. The kingdom was all but destroyed in the twelfth and thirteenth centuries. Ghana was absorbed into the kingdom of Melle, then into the Songhay empire.

14

The kingdom of Melle or Manding was another of the great empires of Africa. This country, founded in the seventh century, was located in the area later known as French West Africa. In the eleventh century the king, Baramendana Keita, became a Moslem. He made a religious journey to Mecca. Mecca is the holy city of the Moslems and is located in present-day Arabia. Agreements with other followers of Islam were made by Baramendana Keita. He began trade with neighboring and distant Arab states.

Sundiata Keita, a great hero of the Mandingo people, made the empire stronger. He invaded and conquered Ghana, by then absorbed into the Kingdom of Soso. In the first third of the fourteenth century, the empire was peaceful. Most of the people were farmers, but many were engaged in building and mining. They now held the rich gold mines of Bure. Brick buildings, pyramids, and castles replaced the straw huts.

In 1324 Gunga Musa, the ruler of Melle, made a religious trip to Mecca. His was perhaps the greatest journey ever to leave Africa on a pilgrimage to Mecca. It is reported that Gunga Musa had a caravan of 60,000 people. The greater part of the caravan was made up of soldiers. There were servants dressed in brocade and silk tunics. Five hundred servants marched ahead carrying staffs of pure gold. Food was prepared by special cooks for the king and his friends. Gunga Musa took with him gold loaded on the backs of 80 camels. His fame spread to the Middle East and as far away as Western Europe. The power of the Melle was at its height. But in the fifteenth century, the kingdom began to decline. The attacks by the Songhay and the Mossi lessened the power of Melle.

SONGHAY

During the period 700 to 1335 A.D., the kingdom of Songhay came into being. About 100 A.D. the people lived in an area along the Niger River. The capital was called Gao. This kingdom had great warriors and great statesmen. Their leaders extended the power of Songhay to Timbukutu, the zone lakes, and Walata.

The rise of Songhay was due to good leadership. One of the greatest leaders to appear in Africa was Sonni Ali. He had been captured by Gunga Musa, the Manding. However, he escaped and reached Songhay. He reorganized the army and defeated the Manding. He made the Songhay independent.

The new ruler founded a ruling family called the

Sonni and took the name of Sonni Ali. Sonni Ali was the first to use a navy in warfare. Boats had been used before in wars. However, Sonni Ali was the first to plan and use a navy for conquest and defense of the Niger River.

Sonni Ali was drowned while crossing a river. He was one of the most effective conquerors and organizers of Africa. Although he had accepted the Mohammedan faith, he was an animist at heart. An animist believes that all things have good or evil spirits. These spirits must be satisfied so that man will not be disturbed by the evil ones. Sonni Ali knew that he could not build an empire if the people were divided on religion. He did not make religion a state question. Instead, he built his empire on loyalty to the government.

In 1493, the ruling family of Sonni was overthrown. Askia Mohammed became Songhay's most brilliant ruler. He strengthened the empire and encouraged learning. The people were prosperous. In 1494, the Songhay was the largest and most powerful state in the history of West Africa. But civil wars and massacres followed the reign of Askia. The empire began to decline.

Smaller empires were found to the south and east of the Songhay empire. The Mossi states formed one of these. It was made up of several kingdoms. Its rulers were like the other early African kings. Their governments were much the same.

Each state had several kingdoms, and their rulers pledged allegiance to the emperor. The empire was made up of provinces. The rulers of these provinces lived at the court of the emperor. They were like our present-day comptroller and general of the army. Other ministers served with them. Among these were the collector of taxes, the chief of the servants, and others. The governors of the provinces ruled their areas with courts of ministers like those of the central government.

The emperor had pages, guards, and servants. Everything was done to the tune of the flute or the beat of the drum. Every morning the emperor had a report from his ministers on the state of the country. Together they made plans for its progress. In the evening, matters of public order and criminal justice were handled. This had much in common with the beginnings of our present-day system of trial by jury.

These smaller states seldom tried to conquer other territories. However, in 1333 A.D., they took Timbuktu. Usually they stayed at home and fought to keep their land from being invaded. The Mossi never became Moslems, and in general West Africa was not greatly influenced by foreign cultures.

The Afno city-states of Hausa were to the east of Songhay. Gober was known for its cotton goods. Kano was the cultural center, controlled by the scholars of Islam. Kateena was rich in farm lands and had a great army. Zaria was a commercial center. It had an efficient queen who had power over the other Afno cities. These states never united to form an empire.

The Bornu people lived on both sides of Lake Chad east of the Afno city-states. These people were a mixture of many races. Some were Blacks; others were a mixture of Semites, Berbers, Moroccans, and Arabs.

There is little known about Africa below the equator. There were apparently some small states there. None of these states reached the size of Ghana, Melle, or the Songhay. There are huge stone ruins much farther southeast in Africa at Zimbabwe. It is said that they were built about the same time that Ghana became great. It is not known who built them or what stage of civilization was reached. It is in this area that some scholars believe there was a great civilization at the height of Egyptian power.

CHAPTER 2

Interesting Peoples of Africa

Ancient African history is still a mystery to us. The many tribes living below the Sahara did not know how to write. This is why there is no record of their past. What we do know about the tribes has been learned from the stories, songs, and dances handed down from one generation to the next. However, examples of native culture do remain. The Bushmen left rock paintings of animals and religious ceremonies. The West Africans left bronze figures.

We know less about Africa below the Sahara than perhaps about any other part of the world. Africa below the Sahara was a very hard place to explore. But, from some of the artifacts that have been found, we are sure that the people of this land had an advanced culture. The African way of life was not much different from that of others in ancient times. All peoples had blended and intermarried. They borrowed ways of doing things from each other. We do know that the African was the first to learn the use of iron.

Many scientists think that the first true man appeared in Africa. Dr. Louis Leakey found the remains of a creature who walked upright on an island in Lake Victoria. Many other remains of prehistoric, man-like creatures have been found in East Africa and South Africa. Some of these remains date back more than a million years. We know more about man's giant step toward a better way of life as he entered the Stone Age. Many kinds of men developed and found better ways of living.

In Africa, a great many people live near the equator. This is the hottest part of the continent. Heavy rains and year-round heat make the plants grow in abundance, so the jungles are very thick. Tall trees have thick vines growing on them. The forests are so dense that it is hard to open a path and keep it open. The forests have an abundance of animals, natural crops, and fruits. Because of this abundance, there is less struggle for man to live.

Since the weather is always warm, the people do

not need much in the way of clothes. Because of the heat, they do not need as much food as people in other climates. Most of the work has to be done in the early morning or late afternoon because the middle of the day is too hot. Those Africans who live at or near the equator where there is little struggle for life have not made much progress.

Above and below the equator are places that have less rainfall. The climate is not as hot, and plant life is not as abundant. There, it is necessary to grow crops in order to live. People living in the places where they have to plant crops have made more progress. It is necessary for them to control nature in order to have enough food.

The people of Africa living below the Sahara are commonly known as the black race. However, they differ widely. Some differ because they have intermingled with many other peoples. There are those who came from Asia into Egypt. The Egyptians, in turn, went up the Nile into the interior of Africa. In much the same way, people from the interior of Africa went to Egypt and Ethiopia. Some people differ because of the differences in climate. In Northeast Africa, south of Egypt, the people look like both black and white people. They have very dark skin and coarse hair. But their features are like those of white people.

There were in Africa, below the equator, five main native groups of people. The Pygmies lived in the tropical forests near the equator. The Bushmen lived in the Kalahari Desert. The Hottentots lived in South Africa. The Bantu had spread through East Africa. The Bantu were the largest group: they blended with the light-skinned Hamites from the north and the Bushmen from the south. The African people are very different from each other in speech and customs. A West African cannot talk with a Bantu from Kenya because there are many different languages and dialects.

Throughout the entire historic period, Africa has been divided racially and culturally by the Sahara Desert. North of the desert the people have been a blend of Caucasian, African, and Asiatic cultures. South of the desert the people are mostly Negroid. Their way of life remained different. This happened in spite of intrusions from the outside.

The Bushmen

The Bushmen lived as early as the prehistoric period. They were found in South Africa. However, at one time they traveled as far north as Kenya. During the late prehistoric period, they were driven south and forced into less desirable lands by the Bantus.

The Bushmen were called "boshies-men" because

they lived in forests and mountainous places, and "boshie" means little forest. They were a small, slender people, their skin was yellow, and they had slanted eyes. They had an odd clicking speech that set them apart from others. They were very timid and shy, and they called themselves the Harmless People. Because they were not fighters, they were driven away by the Hottentots and the Bantu tribes. They lived on land that no one else wanted.

These people were not farmers. They lived on wild game, desert melons, berries, and roots. As a result, they were a wandering people who searched for food.

Poison arrows were used to hunt their game, so the Bushmen knew a great deal about poisons and their antidotes. The bows were made of wood and were rather small. The arrowheads had a cutting edge. A bone point coated with a deadly poison was placed behind the arrowhead. The sharp edge of the arrow cut the veins of the animal. This permitted the poison to circulate inside the animal more rapidly.

The Bushmen used many disguises to get close to the animals they were hunting. A well-known Bushman painting shows a herd of antelopes with some ostriches. One ostrich, however, has human legs. A stalking trick of the Bushman was to get into an ostrich skin with a stick up through the neck and then work up to the unobservant antelope.

The women had a useful tool called a digging stick. At the end of this hardwood stick was an oval-shaped stone. This tool was used for collecting roots and digging out small animals that lived in the ground.

The Bushmen were rather loosely grouped as tribes speaking the same language. The tribes were made up of bands. These bands were the real groupings for social life. Each band roamed around in its own territory. The Bushmen had no possessions, but lived in caves. The men wore loincloths, and the women wore aprons of soft-tanned hides. There were fur robes, also, to protect them from the cold nights. The women wore colored beads made from ostrich eggs. Ostrich shells were used as water bottles. Two or three mats made up the rest of their belongings.

Each band had a chief who managed the family affairs, helped to settle arguments, and was the keeper of the sacred fire. This sacred fire held a special position. When the gods first gave primitive man fire, a constant watch was kept over it. Man was afraid that the gift might be lost. The sacred fire was a reminder of the days when this watch was kept. All fires in the Bushmen's camp had to be made from the sacred fire.

The bands often broke down into single families. These families roamed alone in search of food. They separated from the band during times when there was not much food to be had. The families would come together after long periods of time. Each man had one wife. Widows and other unattached women were cared for by the best hunters in the bands. Wives were always taken from another band in the same tribe. In camp each family had its own hut and its own cooking fire. Unmarried men and teen-age boys had their own huts.

As a people, the Bushmen had wonderful ability to withstand hardships. They had good eyesight and excellent hearing. They had a folklore and an interest in music. Their folklore consisted of animal tales. They also had skill in drawing men and animals. Wherever the Bushmen lived, caves and rocks were decorated with paintings. Some of these paintings still exist, and they have been divided into two periods. The Earlier Period shows a peaceful and simple life. Nature and religious ceremonies were painted. A Later Period shows paintings that were not so carefully or skillfully done. The scenes are of fights, raids, and ceremonies. The beginnings of rock art in South Africa date from 10,000 to 8,000 B.C.

Not much is known about the Bushmen's religion. They seem to have believed in a Supreme Being.

27

The medicine man worked against evil spirits. He cast spells to protect the people from lions, snakes, scorpions, and the drought. When the Dutch came to South Africa, the Bushmen withdrew to the mountains.

The Bantus

The Bantus were the largest group in Africa. They populated the whole central and southern part of the continent. The word "Bantu" in African means people, and many tribes belonged to the Bantus. Among these were the Zulus, Matabele, Angoni, Bechuana, Basuto, and Kikuyu. Among the Bantu tribes, about two hundred and sixty different languages were spoken. Most of these tribes had kept their valuable traditions except when they had been broken up by war.

The Bantus were farmers. They raised millet, pumpkins, beans, sugar cane, and melons. In their trading, they used cattle instead of money. Their farming was very simple, for they had few tools. Farming was carried on mostly by the women. The men spent their time in warfare, using the spear and shield.

A tribe was made up of clans. One family usually provided the chief or king of the tribe. The oldest member of the ruling family was the chief. The chief of the tribe was the judge, the general of the army, and the high priest. Under him were lesser chiefs of the clans making up the tribes. Under these were the heads of families. Families were organized the same way, with the oldest member serving as the leader. In addition to parents and children, an African family included grandparents, uncles, aunts, and cousins. Members of the family often owned land and other property together. Many tribes believed that the dead could influence the lives of the living; therefore, the families included both living and dead relatives. The leaders had the same power over their families as the chief had over the tribe.

This way of governing was very much like that of the early Greeks and Romans. The Bantu tribes never had a strong central government like those of modern times. They lived in villages of from five to five hundred people. Each village was independent of the other. The head of the village represented the chief of the tribe. The most important village was the one in which the chief lived.

Cattle was the basis of tribal life. A man with many heads of cattle held a high position in the tribe. Cattle was the means by which a man could get a wife. According to Bantu law, a man was allowed as many wives as he could afford. A man gave cattle to his wife's family to make up to them for the loss of her services. The gift of the cattle showed good faith. The wife's father and brothers were anxious for the marriage to succeed. If the marriage failed, the cattle was returned. Family ties were so strong that a man could not marry unless his family liked the bride.

The laws of the tribe were very strict. The individual was not considered. Everything was done for the good of the tribe. Children were taught to obey the laws. The boys were trained as warriors, and the girls were trained to be wives. When the children were fully developed, they were taken from their families. They lived in separate villages, where the boys were taught to withstand pain and the girls were taught every aspect of marriage.

Africans loved music and dancing. The beat of the drum was to be heard at times of feasting and rejoicing. Men and women sang as they worked. They used drums to call to war. There were ancient songs for special occasions. The dancers dramatized love, war, birth, and death.

Eventually the Boers and the British took the land away from the Bantus.

The Hottentots

The Hottentots appeared in South Africa later than the Bushmen. They were a small people: their average height was about five feet three inches. The

Hottentots had long heads and coarse hair like that of the Bushmen. They had pale reddish-yellow skin and high cheek bones. Hottentot girls were attractive as children. They married young, often at eleven or twelve years of age.

Hottentot people had high spirits. They were usually cheerful and hopeful. Merrymaking, singing, and dancing were part of their lives. When the new moon appeared, members of the tribe sang and danced all night. The Hottentots loved the heavenly bodies and gave them names. These people had very great imaginations. Like the Bushmen, they were sturdy and could endure many hardships.

The Hottentots kept cattle, sheep, and goats. Although they used poisoned arrows for hunting, they did not depend on this for food. They had milk and the meat of their cattle and sheep for food. They also ate roots, wild fruits, and vegetables. Skins and animal furs were used for clothes. The Hottentots wandered from place to place to find grazing land for their cattle.

When the Hottentots stayed in one place for a length of time, they built huts. Their huts were made of sticks bound together and covered with mats and rushes. The women did most of the heavy work. The milking of the cows and goats was done by the women.

Each band had a head man or chief. These leaders had no real authority. But members of the family had great respect for each other. There was also a strong relationship between a man and his mother's brother. Religion was based on ancestor worship. An important religious ceremony was held in November and December. It was a rain-making ceremony carried on when the rains were due.

With the coming of the Dutch, the Hottentots adapted themselves to European ways.

The Pygmies

The Pygmies are a people who live in the Congo jungle. They appeared before the Stone Age. The jungle was near the equator, and the climate was hot. Rainfall was heavy, so plant life grew very fast and the plants were large. The trees were tall. Trunks of the trees grew across or over others. All the spaces between them were filled with moss, vines, thorns, poisonous mushrooms, and the like. There were ants, unbelievably large, that would bite. Beetles and spiders were also enormous, and there were huge crocodiles and leopards. The crocodiles were fifteen feet long. The leopards were nine to ten feet long.

Here lived the Pygmies. These people looked like

dwarfs, for they did not grow any taller than four feet six inches. Although they had short legs, their arms were long. The Pygmies had yellow-brown skin, round heads, and curly, reddish-brown hair. Their stomachs stuck out like those of little children. They were a sturdy group, kind, brave, and happy.

The Pygmies lived by hunting and fishing. They did not farm. They hunted with bows and arrows, and some used spears. They killed antelopes, monkeys, birds, elephants, and buffaloes. They also trapped some of these animals.

The bows and arrows of the Pygmies were small. The arrow was made of reed. One end had a sharp point which was coated with a deadly poison. A feather was inserted at the other end. This kept the arrow steady. Traps that had been cleverly hidden were used to catch leopards and other big game. These traps had been set around the clearing where the Pygmies lived. All night long a big fire was kept burning. The leopard would prowl around the fire. His eyes would become blinded by the flames. When one paw was caught, the Pygmies killed him with their spears. The skin was cleaned and used for clothing.

The Pygmies needed plenty of meat in order to live. They killed the elephant, buffalo, hippopotamus, and the giant hog. Once the animal had fallen to the bottom of a deep pit, he was killed easily. Many hundreds of the pits used to trap big game were always ready. Some of these had been dug by the Pygmies' ancestors.

Pygmies lived in small roaming bands. There were several of these bands, and each went throughout its own territory. They had many thousand square miles each. These people had lived in the forests for many hundreds of years. Their homes were in the great trees in the heart of the jungle. They spoke the language of the nearest tribe.

The oldest member of the band served as its leader. He led the hunters on the trail and told them when and how to attack. He was the first to go into dangerous situations and the last to leave. The leader or chief took care of the whole band. He saw that they were well fed. He did all the trading with the Bantu. He gave his consent for all marriages. He named newborn children. He took care of burying the dead.

The men made bows and arrows, spears, knives, and clay pots. They prepared gourds to be used as water bottles and water pipes. They gathered wild tobacco, fruits, and mushrooms. The men drew out the poison from the roots of plants. This poison was used on the tips of their arrows and spears. They gathered bark from trees and cut it into the proper size for clothing. The women boiled this bark, then the men beat it with ivory hammers. When the bark was thin and soft, the women dyed it. The chips of certain trees gave them dyes of dark yellow, brown, and purple.

The men spent most of their time tracking, trapping, and hunting. The meat that was brought back was for all. Meat which was left over was smoked and later traded to the Bantu for iron, bananas, beans, manioc, and sweet potatoes. The women took care of the children. They carried the water and kept the huts in good condition.

The Pygmies were the most backward of all the African people. Other cultures had not gotten through to them. The Pygmies knew the jungle well. They lived by instinct and customs handed down to them from hundreds of years ago.

What of the Pygmies now? They are mostly dependent on the large Blacks. But these Blacks have their own hunters. They do not need the Pygmies to supply them with meat. The Pygmies made good scouts. They were able to give villages warnings of enemy war parties. But the usefulness of the Pygmies is coming to an end.

CHAPTER 3

Life Among
The Peoples of Africa

The Farmers and Cattlemen

The people of Africa below the Sahara were not all farmers. Some raised crops; others raised cattle and sheep. Farming could not be carried on in all areas. Some hunting tribes changed to keeping cattle and sheep. The Bantus south of Kenya were farmers, while the Sudanic and East African tribes raised cattle. The West Africans were farmers also. Cattlemen and farmers lived side by side and exchanged their products. Some tribes practiced both farming and cattle raising.

The farmers usually had great and permanent kingdoms. In places where the rainfall was heaviest, goats, chickens, dogs, and hogs were the animals kept. The farmers raised bananas, yams, and taro. In the places where rainfall was less heavy, maize, manioc, millet, sorghum, peanuts, and ground nuts were raised.

Land did not belong to any one person: it belonged either to the whole village or to a whole family. When the land belonged to the entire village, each person or family might have permission to use part of it.

Land was cleared by chopping down trees and burning the low bushes. The ashes were used as fertilizer. Since these farmers had no plows, they used a short-handled tool like a hoe. A person had to bend almost in half to use this tool. Seeds were planted and carefully tended. The land had to be weeded often, as weeds grew very fast. At harvest time the grain was harvested, threshed, milled, and stored. Other fruits and grains were made into fermented drinks. Cotton was made into thread and cloth.

Once the banana plants began to grow, they would produce fruit for twenty-five or thirty years. This made permanent settlements possible. So many bananas grew that many people could be fed. The women did all the farming.

Basketry and weaving were done in the farming areas. The weaving of cloth was done most skillfully in the northwestern section. In the eastern and southern sections, bark cloth took the place of woven cloth. Bark cloth was made from the trees of the *ficus* family.

Clearing the land was very hard work, especially in the rain forest area. But the crops raised did not make the land poor rapidly, and the farmers were able to stay in the same place longer. In areas where there was less rain, the land could be used for only two or three years. Then the land had to be left un-planted for ten to twenty years. The weeds were too difficult for the farmers to handle. They found it easier to leave the fields. When the larger plants grew, they covered the land and killed the weeds. Under these conditions villages had to move every twenty to thirty years. Owning land was not important. The men of a tribe banded together in a group to clear new land. All of the farming groups organized their men in this way.

Another group of farmers was those who kept cat-tle. Other animals, especially sheep, were kept in small numbers. Cattle was the most valuable posses-sion. Work with them was done by men. Although the Hottentot women milked the cows, other African people scorned this practice.

The bride price or lobola was always paid in cat-tle. A man was called wealthy according to the size of his herd. A man loved his cattle. Even those who had several hundred knew every animal belonging to them. Cattle were kept in pens during the night. They grazed during the day, and the boys of the tribe were herders. The cattle were milked and bled morning and night. A small bow and arrow was driven into one of the veins of the neck. This started the bleeding. A quart or two of blood was drawn off and the wound closed. This seemed not to cause the animal any pain. Blood was an important part of the diet of all people who lived by hunting.

The tribes that raised cattle did not make a practice of hunting. They hunted lions and other animals to keep these beasts away from the cattle. Often they shared their land with hunting tribes. The cattlemen considered the hunting tribes inferior.

The religious beliefs and practices of these cattlemen were simple. They acknowledged a Supreme Being. They did not indulge in the elaborate rites and ceremonies of the farming tribes. They worshipped gods or ancestors only in times of trouble. Sometimes animal sacrifices were made. Human sacrifices were rarely performed.

The cattlemen lived in small krāals. A krāal may be a single hut or a group of huts surrounded by a fence. The fence is made of stakes driven into the ground and pointed at the top. Each krāal was occupied by a family. The family usually included wives, sons, and sons' wives. The cattle pen was in the center of this group of houses. This was done to protect the cattle from raids, as most of the African cattlemen were very warlike. They often were at war with their farming neighbors. There developed numerous states in which the cattlemen ruled over the farmers.

The Sudanese and East African people had a simple form of government. Several clans and sub-clans were formed. Each group was controlled by a chief or a medicine man whose main duty was the making of rain. All the boys of a certain age were initiated into manhood at the same time. Then they served as a unit in the army.

Bantu tribes lived on the plateau south of Kenya. They raised cattle to a large extent. However, they depended much more on farming than the Sudanese and East African cattlemen. Farming as it is known in other countries was late in coming to Africa.

In Egypt, the Nile Valley was very fertile. When the Nile overflowed its banks, rich mud was left. When the floods were over, the people got the ground ready for planting. The Egyptians did not have farm tools as we have today. Their tools were very crude: the plows were wooden and only

41

scratched the soil. Big lumps of earth had to be broken up by a wooden hoe. The farmer sowed his seed over this crudely plowed ground. Flocks of sheep were driven over it to tread the seed into the ground. Except for irrigation, the crops did not need tending until time for harvest.

Grain was cut with a sickle. The grain was loaded on donkeys and taken to the threshing floor. Here it was trod on by donkeys driven back and forth over it. Later, oxen were used for this purpose. Then the grain was thrown up into the air. The grain fell straight down and the chaff was blown forward. In this way the grain was separated from the chaff. The grain was taken to the granary where it was measured and stored. Wheat, barley, and millet were the leading grains of Egypt. Little is known of the vegetables grown in olden times; it is known that melons, onions, and cucumbers were grown. We also know that the grape vine was tended.

Cattle raising was also carried on. The Egyptians knew how to breed fine oxen and cows, and the cattle raisers were a class by themselves. In the summer time they drove the cattle up north where the pastures were good. The average Egyptian disliked these men because they let their hair grow long and wore beards. They lived in huts and did not dress well. The people in the towns laughed at them.

The cattle raisers spent their free time weaving reeds into mats. They wove boats from the same plant. In the fall, they went back to their homes. At home, the owners looked over their stock. Some owners had as many as 1300 cows as well as other cattle. Large flocks of sheep were also kept, and there were many goats. Only in the New Empire period were a few pigs seen because pigs were thought to be unclean.

The whole civilization of Egypt was based on farming and cattle raising. However, the farmer and the cattleman had no social standing. The land was owned by rich noblemen who got all the profit from farming. The ancient peasants worked without enjoying the fruits of their labor.

The Builders

In early Africa, the houses were different from those we know today. The homes of the native Africans were huts with thatched roofs. Some of the houses were built of ebony or mahogany. These were hard woods, for termites would have eaten up the softer woods. In the places where there was heavy rainfall, houses were built up high. This was done to keep them above the rising water. The homes of the tribal chiefs and the wealthy were

43

bigger and better than the others. The houses were arranged in clusters or according to a certain design. Many of the African tribes were wandering tribes. These people did not build permanent homes.

The Egyptians built homes that were not as strong and solid as their tombs. The houses were built for coolness. The walls were thin so that air could circulate. The houses were made of stucco, mud brick, or wood. The outsides of the houses were decorated in gay colors. Bright carpets and matting covered the inside walls.

The wealthy Egyptian had a wall built around his home. A gate opened into a court. A hall off the court led to the dining room. This was the largest and most important room in the house. Another hall led to the bedrooms. The kitchen, store rooms, and servant quarters were separated from the main house. Sometimes the houses were two stories high. A stairway led to the roof. The roof was used for many things after the sun went down. The wealthy had many buildings. One building was for the women, another had rooms for receiving guests.

The pharoah built his own city. He had many buildings; all were enclosed by a wall. Many samples of Egyptian furniture were found in tombs. There were chairs, couches, tables, and beds.

The poor Egyptian had a tiny hut built of mud

brick. The roof was usually made of palm leaves. The poorest had only one room, while others had two or three rooms. Once or twice in a hundred years the rains would wash these huts away. When the rain was over, the family would build a new house of sun-dried brick in the same place. Sometimes the houses were leveled to the ground because it was easier to build a new one than clean the old one. The poor today live much the same as those of other centuries.

In the times of Menes, the city of Memphis was built to protect it from Asiatic invaders. Menes built a high embankment across the Nile. The river was turned into a new course farther east. He filled in the old river bed and built a wall around the city. A line of forts was built along the Gulf of Suez.

From the earliest times, the Egyptian kings were builders. They built tombs and temples, and, during the Old Empire, the tombs took the form of pyramids. Some pyramids were small and some were very large. Three of these pyramids are so large that they overshadow all the rest. These are called the "three Pyramids of Gizeh." Khufu built the largest and his son Khafre built the one next in size. The smallest of the three was built by Menkure.

The bottom of the largest pyramid covers thirteen acres. It was once 482 feet high. It is a mass of stone.

It is said that it took 100,000 men twenty years to build it. The rulers who built these tombs wished to keep their names alive. They also wished to keep their bodies from harm after death.

Three kinds of stones were used in the building of a pyramid. The inner part was made of limestone, found on the site. The next layers were built in the form of steps. These were made of stone brought from across the river. This stone was brought from the quarries to the east. Beautiful granite was used for the outer layer. This was found in the south and floated down the river when the water was high. The granite was polished until it shone like a mirror.

One of the Egyptian temples, called the Temple of Dendar, has been removed, stone by stone, to be rebuilt one day as part of the Metropolitan Museum in New York. It should be a strange and beautiful sight.

For several hundred years, the Mohammedans occupied Egypt. They took large quantities of granite from the pyramids. They built mosques and buildings in Cairo. The granite from the Great Pyramid was removed. This left the second layer, the one of steps, bare. Today, many tourists climb to the top of the huge pyramid. The pyramids with granite coverings are no longer smooth. The weather has made this covering rough. The polish has been dulled, and in certain lights they shine like gold. Inside the pyramids were rooms for the bodies of the kings and their families. There were also rooms for friends who came to worship. After his death, an Egyptian king was worshipped as a god.

Every man in Egypt had to have some trade. He had to work at it and no other. Often he received food, but no wages. Large numbers of laborers belonged to the state or to the temples. Some of these men chiseled the granite, others decorated the tombs. All lived in mud huts.

The Metal Workers

The use of iron began in Africa. The African natives were skilled workmen. Blacksmiths and other iron workers were found in many parts of Africa. The native blacksmith smelted his ore with simple bellows and a charcoal fire. He made implements such as knives, saws, and axes. The Africans also exported iron for many years.

In addition, brass and gold were cast by the lost wax process. First, a clay core was molded by the craftsman. This core was in the shape of the object he wished to make. When the core was thoroughly dried, he covered it with a layer of wax. The details which he used were modeled and cut in the casting.

47

Lastly, the core and wax layer were put in a clay shell and the whole mold fired. The wax melted and ran out. This left a hole in which the melted metal could be poured. After the metal had set, the outer shell was broken off. The inner core was dug out, leaving a hollow metal form. This method has never been improved upon for delicate metal work. It is still used by artists today in casting small bronze figures. Africans have not been interested in their mineral wealth, except for iron. Other metals were used chiefly for ornamental and artistic work.

Basketry and mat weaving were done in the farming areas. The weaving of cloth was done in the northwestern part of Africa, below the Sahara. This was a great farming area. In the eastern and southern parts bark cloth was made. Pottery, which was used for cooking, was also made. In most of the farming areas wood carvings were made. Many beautiful wood carvings were produced in the great kingdoms of West Africa. Ivory was used for ornaments and charms, and it was carved with great skill. Ornamental metal work was produced in West Africa. Some tribes made elaborate objects. They usually used brass, which was cast by the lost wax method. The Ashanti tribe was famous for small brass figures. In Benin, bronze and copper implements and art objects show the great skill of the smiths. In our

48

own century, many great artists of the Western world have been influenced by the strength and beauty of these sculptures. Many tribes, including those of Yoruba, Melle, and Jenne, made ornamental objects of silver and gold. The Africans were once the greatest metal workers in the world. They were the first to smelt iron and use the forge. The discovery of iron is an outstanding contribution of the African people.

The Egyptians had learned to mix their copper and tin to make bronze by 1500 B.C. The introduction of the bellows made the work of smelting easier. The Egyptians knew most ordinary metals used today. Gold was more plentiful in Egypt than in any other ancient civilization. It was pounded out of gold-bearing quartz, which was found in the local granite. It was also sent from Nubia as tribute. Silver was rare and, therefore, was greater in value than gold. The work of the Egyptian jewelers can hardly be bettered today. All of the modern methods for working with gold and enamel were known to them.

The Egyptians, successful in working with bronze, used this metal for everyday articles. Iron knives and weapons were made. Bronze was worked for statues of the gods and other ceremonial objects. Gold was often used for this purpose too. The gold-

49

smith was an important person in Egyptian society. He made statues of the gods and cut and set jewelry for the noblemen. Bracelets, anklets, chains, and scarabs were widely worn. The goldsmiths were skillful in their art, which can be seen in many museums.

The Traders

Trading in Africa below the Sahara was carried on among the tribes. Each tribe had its own specialty. It either hunted, farmed, raised cattle, or engaged in industrial arts. They traded with each other to get things they did not produce themselves. Tradesmen traveled from one tribe to another to exchange their wares. When the tradesmen returned home, they sold the goods to their tribesmen. Some merchants from West Africa went as far as the Mediterranean; others went as far east as Egypt. They exchanged their goods for products from other parts of the world. Kings and emperors traveled to Egypt to trade goods. Over these routes African culture traveled. Thus Africa gave of her culture and received culture from others.

During the 1400's the Portuguese made trips to the western coast of Africa. They discovered gold there. This part of West Africa was then called the

Gold Coast. The Portuguese bought gold and ivory from the Gold Coast traders.

The women in the more advanced countries engaged in trade. Their business was conducted in the market place. Every woman tried to produce more food than her family would need. She took this extra food to market.

Long distance expeditions were made. Instead of money, the tradesmen used blocks of salt, copper, iron tools, and weapons. The courie shell was the standard unit of value in many places in Africa. These shells came from the Maldive Islands off the coast of India. When the first Europeans arrived in West Africa, millions of these shells were in circulation. They were traded across the continent. This proves how widespread African trade was.

The old Egyptian markets were noisy little squares. Cattle were grouped in the center waiting for a buyer. Peasants, fishermen, and craftsmen sat in front of the houses showing their wares. These wares were either in large baskets made of rush or on low tables. The customer went past and examined the goods. The customer carried something he had made, which he then used for exchange. What he used for money may have been a new tool, a mat, or rings of copper, silver, or gold. The

51

butcher, baker, and small tradesman preferred to trade for metal. Most of the tradesmen were manufacturers. They had apprentices or workmen who worked for them.

The Egyptians were able to build ships. This made it possible for them to take long voyages. As far back as 1493 B.C., Hatshepsut sent five ships of thirty rowers each to Punt. These ships went by way of the Red Sea. They returned with valuable woods, incense, ebony, and ivory. The Egyptians probably began by sailing on the Nile. They started going on sea voyages to find wood because Egypt was a land without forests. One of the first places the ships went to was the mountain country of Sinai.

CHAPTER 4

Social Living

The Family

The family was the basis of African life. It was a common practice to trace the relationship of families through the mother instead of the father. But some tribes admitted only male relationships. In tribes that were based only on female relationships, the brother of the mother was the chief of the family. In tribes that did not follow this practice, the chief was the real father. With either group, the people making up the family were all the descendants of the same ancestor. All the men of the same family lived together. They brought their wives to live with their family. The village was made up of several families, and each lived in a separate area. The oldest male was the head of the family.

A wife was not a member of her husband's family. After marriage, she was still a part of her own family. The husband was expected to pay his wife's family for taking her away. This was called the "bride price."

Only rich men could have more than one wife. At the first marriage, the chief of the family paid all the expenses. The husband had to meet all of the expenses for the second wife. Religion played a part in deciding how many wives a man could have. The African religion set no limits on the number of wives a man could have. When the Moslems invaded Africa, they set the limit at four.

The clan was made up of all the families that had the same ancestors. The entire clan lived in the same village. Sometimes one or more families would go to another place to live. If there had been no quarrel, these families still thought of themselves as part of the clan. The clan was united in war, work, and religious activities. The feeling of brotherhood ran throughout the family and clan. All were equal. Everything was done for the good of the many and not for the few. Everybody worked, and everybody enjoyed the results of their labor. There were no very rich and no very poor families. The land was free to all. However, things like cattle could belong to one person. And all property was protected by the tribe. Everything was thought of as belonging to the chief. The owner felt that he was using what belonged to the chief. What anyone had beyond his share was divided among his relatives after he died.

In the family, children were taught to show great respect for their parents and their elders. Members of the clan showed great respect towards the heads of the clan, kings, and officials. The rights of the wife were watched over carefully. The rules regarding her rights were worked out with great care. The first wife was the head of the woman's half of the family. The husband's time was divided equally among his wives. This was a definite number of days. During this period, the wife had all rights to her husband. She could claim a share of any money which he might make while he was with her. The choice of a new wife had to be approved by all the others. Sometimes a man's wives urged him to marry a certain woman. There were few quarrels among the wives. Their rights were very clear and the husband's duties were very definite.

In the family, each wife spent her allotted time with her husband in caring for the home. She cooked and cared for the children of the group. This left the other wives free to work in the fields while others sold their goods in the markets. The husband was supposed to be the master of the house. However, only a very brave man could oppose his wives when they presented a united front. The tie between father and son was not close. There was little love between brothers, especially those by different wives.

The African family was a closely knit unit. This was shown by the ceremonies and customs that took place when a member of the family died. Ceremonies and rituals were the sacred duty of the members of the family. The grave was not closed until every member of the family had made some offering.

The family was the main unit of the social structure in early Africa and as such, had great power over its members. Although there were social classes, families, not individuals, made up the classes. At the top was the nobility. These were families whose members could prove that they were offspring of free men. They had the right to places and positions of respect. The majority of Africans were the common people. They found it hard to prove that they came from a long line of ancestors. These people might have had a good clan name but they could not prove their right to it. They could not prove themselves fit for a position in the upper class. At the bottom of the ladder were those who were slaves, war captives, disgraced people, or criminals. Wealth belonged only to the upper class.

Work did not lower the family's standing. However, the kind of work they did determined their standing. Farming was the highest of all occupations. After that came the cattle raising, hunting, fishing, building, trade, gold mining, and the making of such things as soap, oil, and beer. There were differences from tribe to tribe. In some tribes, farming might be the highest occupation, in others cattle raising. Everywhere families received respect according to the kinds of work they did. All people were considered necessary to society. They were respected for what they gave to better society.

A member of a family of another occupation might decide to farm. In time, he could win respect and admiration as a farmer. Then he would be regarded as a member of the class of noble farmers. As in almost every society in the world, power and wealth could take the place of noble birth.

Some Africans had slaves. Slaves were mostly persons captured in war. Some slaves were criminals or disgraced persons. Slaves were the property of the chief of the tribe or the head of the family. By law, slaves were property like animals or furniture. Often they were trusted by their master and enjoyed some privileges. Some were sold, others were used as sacrifices by the king in the worship of his ancestors. The children of slaves could not be sold. They were part of the family's property. Often they were set free by their masters.

Love and Marriage

The African boy married for the good of his tribe. The marriage was arranged, and the young people had nothing to do with it. The boy gave a number of cows, goats, sheep, or cattle to the parents of the girl he wished to marry. He did not buy his wife: these gifts were a pledge that the wife would be treated well. If the wife were not treated well, she could return to her father. The gifts were not returned.

The marriage ceremony was celebrated with dancing. Everyone took part in this dancing. The dancing was without rhythm, a kind of jumping done by the guests. Members of the family danced more gracefully. For music they used drums, horns, and reed and stringed instruments.

Women did most of the work so that the men could hunt or make war on other tribes. In certain tribes the husband usually paid close attention to one of his wives. She ran his home, while the other wives were treated as servants. Some tribes did not allow a man to have more than one wife.

When there were tribal wars, many soldiers were

killed. Then there were more women than men. As a rule, a woman had to attach herself to some man. The custom of having more than one wife meant that there were no unmarried women. The women then produced more male children who grew up to help protect the tribe. The women were true to their husbands. If they were not, strict laws punished them. They were either crippled, disfigured, or put to death.

Religion and Morals

The religion of the early African was ancestor worship. He believed that man's spirit could never die. He also thought that the spirits of his ancestors had great power over his life. It was believed that the spirit that lived in a relative was made into a god upon death. The spirit continued to live and took an interest in the family. The African believed that man could talk face-to-face with the spirits of the dead. An old custom on the Gold Coast was to take food and drink to the grave. Then the relatives spoke to the spirit. It was believed that the spirit of the dead stayed nearby day and night.

The African looked beyond his life to a world hereafter. He believed that he would meet every member of his family again, especially those whom he loved. With this in mind, he went through life in a carefree manner. There was special worship of early ancestors, as those who had been dead the longest were more powerful than those who had died recently. A high regard was held for those spirits which lived in the family land—in the trees, rocks, and sky above the village. It was believed, too, that the ancestors could harm the family. The African sought to change the behavior of the spirits by prayers and sacrifices.

Religion was much more important among the farmers than among the cattlemen. The ancestors were believed to be present all the time. They helped their descendants, and they also punished them for any moral slips. The male ancestors were more feared than loved. There were also other gods. These were connected with nature, such as the Sun God and the River God.

Religion was controlled by the priests. The king was at the head of this group. However, the king did not usually interfere. The priests shared their duties with the medicine man. Working in this way, the priests treated both mind and body. The training of a priest began in early childhood. He was sent to another village for this training for a number of years. He studied religion and the use of herbal remedies.

The end of his training was marked by an exciting dance. At this time, a magic power was said to have come upon him. Some of these medico-priests were known to cure diseases that have puzzled many European doctors. They were expert in the use of the herbs and worked very secretly. The people believed that these priests could do many things that seemed impossible. The office of the priest was sacred among the Africans.

The priest was the ruler of the family. He was the oldest living member of the descendants of the first ancestor. He had inherited the earthly rights and privileges of the ancestor. The priest had control over the family grounds, waters, and air. He also had the power to hold the ceremonies of worship. The temple of worship could be any building set aside for this purpose. This building held the holy objects, such as the bones of the dead, sacred pieces of work, rocks or metal, and statuettes of objects to be worshipped. Bells or rattles were used to call forth the spirits and the worshippers. The blood of victims, chickens, sheep, goats, or human beings were offered as sacrifices to satisfy the gods. It was never a common practice to sacrifice human beings in Africa. However, in some areas, prisoners and captives were sacrificed in worship of the various gods. The pouring out of palm wine, beer, or some other alcoholic drink was offered in some forms of worship.

There was a belief in magic of all sorts. It was practiced on a wide scale. The magician of Africa created ways and means for individuals to get things they desired.

The medicine man was usually a person who was easily emotional. The job gave him an important place in society. It also paid well. Children were watched for signs of an ability to do this kind of work. To be successful in this field, a medicine man had to understand people. The medicine man believed that he had great powers and great wisdom. He knew many remedies for common diseases. A study of healing practices of African medicine men would surely add knowledge to our own medical practices.

The medicine man knew both good and bad magic. He could kill as well as heal. He was ready to provide evil charms and taught people how to use them. But this was only a small part of his duties. The sorcerer, though, was found everywhere in Africa. He practiced only evil magic, and his witchcraft was directed against individuals as well as families or clans. Whenever sorcerers were discovered, they were killed. It was believed that a person could be a sorcerer or witch without knowing it. Persons who were found and accused of witchcraft by the medicine men would usually confess. They allowed themselves to be executed without protest.

One of the most important duties of the medicine man was the making of fetishes. A fetish is any thing supposed to have magic power. These were thought to bring good or evil fortune. The fetishes were made of materials taken from plants or animals. The most powerful fetishes were made of human blood, bones, or organs.

Each village had a fetish. It was prepared by the medicine man at the time the village was built. It was carried to the new place whenever the village moved. It was supposed to protect the health and good fortune of the village. Sacrifices and prayers were made to it: it was treated like a god. The fetish was supposed to bring good fortune in hunting, fishing, and farming. There were sacrifices and ceremonies to the village fetish. Each person also had his own fetish. Some were worn, others were kept in the houses.

Many natives put great trust in the power of magic. It was thought that this blind faith in the foretelling of the future by sorcerers was partly responsible for the lack of progress in Africa. The practice of casting magical spells and the use of powders kept the people from using their own imagination and skill in meeting problems.

Men who belonged to the farming tribes had secret societies. These societies were religious groups that were organized for social control. Each society had its masks and costumes, in which they gave occasional public performances. Women, children, and men who were not members were supposed to believe that these masked dancers were heavenly beings. The dancers killed anyone who discovered who they really were. These secret societies had signs and passwords, and members took an oath to help each other. These societies united an area where there was no government. The members could travel safely. However, where the government was strong secret societies were frowned upon. In some areas they were forbidden. Anyone discovered belonging to one of these societies was killed.

The activities of these societies differed from place to place. Their main task seemed to have been the enforcement of local customs. Wives and others who did not behave were likely to be beaten or killed by the masked members.

The Africans had one code of law and ethics when dealing with outsiders. They had a different code in dealing with their own kind. Africans believed that telling a lie was a sin. It was a criminal act to disturb the property of another. Those found guilty were punished by a fine, a jail sentence, or, sometimes, death. The native Africans did not need locks and safes. The moral laws of the Hebrews and those of certain Africans were somewhat similar. The Kaffirs of South Africa had laws similar to those of the Hebrews.

Education

There is little information before the sixteenth century about the African states below the Sahara. We do know that the Africans had a system of education. But there were no schools as we know them today. At an early age, the boys were educated or trained by an older man. Girls were trained by an older woman. Both boys and girls were carefully taught hygiene and care of the body.

The young African boy was taught to care for the young goats. He also began to learn how to farm. Later, the boy had to care for larger animals until finally he learned to care for large numbers of cattle.

At an early age, the girls were taught how to take care of the home. They began by providing the family with water. They were taught how to clean the house, pound the corn, and cook the food. The girls were prepared by the older woman for motherhood. They also learned the duty of wives to their husbands. This kind of training was continued until they reached the age of marriage. Then lessons ended with a ceremony. This ceremony included dancing, which was part of the training. In order to get ready for this dance, the girls painted their faces in many colors.

Askia Muhammed ruled in the kingdom of Songhay from 1493 to 1529. He spent a great deal of his time encouraging learning. Schools were begun and encouraged. Gao, Walata, Timbuktu, and Jenne became centers of learning. The most learned scholars of West Africa could be found there. Scholars from Asia and Europe also went there to study and exchange ideas. White scholars, like El-Akit, and black scholars, like Bagayogo, were educated at Timbuktu. Among the subjects taught at the University of Sankore were grammar, geography, law, literature, and surgery.

In the fifteenth century, the Afno or Hausa people had seven states. These states were joined under the kings of Kebbi. Katsena became a center of learning, where law and theology were studied. Here also the language of the people was refined. Today these seven states are known as Nigeria.

Literature

In early Africa, there were many languages and dialects. The Bushmen tribes spoke different languages according to where they lived. The Bantus spoke one hundred and eighty-two languages. The same was true of other tribes. All these languages had dialects. The many languages and dialects made it difficult to have a written language. There were no books of stories, poetry, etc.

Literature was handed down by word of mouth. There were many stories told and retold from one generation to another. Besides many kinds of stories, there were proverbs, poems, love songs, funeral songs, and comic tales. Some of the proverbs show that the African had definite standards of conduct. The following are some examples: "There is no medicine for hate"; "he who injures another brings injury to himself"; "bowing to a dwarf will not prevent your standing erect again"; "the lack of knowledge is darker than night"; "an ignorant man is a slave."

The early African memorized the history, law, and traditions of his people. After the fourteenth century, the educated Moslem blacks used the Arabic alphabet. This made it possible to put oral literature into written form. *Tarikh-El-Soudan* is a history of the Sudan written by Es-Sadi during this time.

67

Oral literature was used to educate the young. It was sometimes used for entertainment. Oral literature, handed down from one generation to another, taught men how to govern the people. For example, the method of holding religious ceremonies was learned in this way. The literature that was finally written in Arabic could be compared favorably with the literature of that time anywhere in the world.

Art

Art is many things. It is commonly thought of as painting and sculpture. But art is the production of beauty in any form. Art appeals to the imagination. Besides painting and sculpture, it is music, poetry, dancing, and dramatics. The African artist did not copy anything. His art came out of his imagination. His way of carving and sculpting were also original. Carving and sculptures were done in wood, stone, and ivory. Large carved tusks of ivory formed part of the Benin altar.

In Benin (900–1440 A.D.), the bronze and brass works showed great skill. They influenced some great artists of the twentieth century. In West Africa, ornamental metal work was highly developed. Some tribes did elaborate iron forging. However, most of the work was done in brass. The finest examples of work in bronze and brass were the heads of the eleventh-century kings of Ife. The Ashanti were famous for their small brass figures and cast gold work. The lost wax process was used.

In Yoruba, terra-cotta pieces showed rare skill and artistic ability. African tribes made many statuettes of people and animals. These were used in religious ceremonies. In all the tribes, artists made images and other symbols for the temples. Some time after 900 B. C. terra-cotta figures began to be made. Terra-cotta was a brownish-red clay that was baked until very hard.

From Timbuktu to the Congo, there was a great deal of work in gold, silver, glass, and clay. The Blacks of Africa decorated their art objects in many ways. There was glazed pottery, spoons and knives beautifully carved, and gold jewelry made in filigree. Mats were richly woven, and cloth and tapestries gave evidence of great artistic ability.

Masks were one of the outstanding features of African art. The masks were used to disguise the wearer. They were also intended to give the wearer the qualities of the being which the mask represented. Often masks were fetishes. Sacrifices were made to them in order to keep their goodwill.

The Africans decorated their houses, palaces, and temples. This kind of decoration improved after the

Moslems invaded Africa south of the Sahara. However, much beauty was seen in the buildings before the invasion of the Moslems.

Music was also very important as a means of expression. The Africans developed musical instruments. Among these were the xylophone, violin, guitar, zither, harp, and flute. The song was used with or without musical instruments. The songs were sometimes sung by two groups, with one group singing answers to the other. There were lullabies, dance songs, work songs, and religious chants.

African songs were often accompanied by drums. The rhythm of the drums for dances were not thought of as music. Some of the drums seemed to talk. The drum was shaped like a cone and covered on the top and bottom by skins. These skins were held in place by leather bands. The drummer hit the drum with a stick. He worked the leather bands so that they sounded like people talking. Messages could be sent rapidly over great distances in this way.

There were many kinds of African dances. Some were for recreational or social occasions. Others were for religious ceremonies. Both music and the dance were part of African culture. In some cases, the dance and music told the story of early African history.

CHAPTER 5

Some Great Men
in Africa's Past

Gunga Musa

Berbers, Arabs, and those of mixed blood crossed into the kingdoms of West Africa and the Sudan. At times these groups drove the Blacks off their lands. At other times the Blacks sent their armies to conquer their neighbors to the north. Often the Blacks added these lands to their own kingdoms. Sometimes other states inhabited by the Berbers, Arabs, and others were allowed to rule themselves. However, they paid tribute to the Blacks.

The most important African states were Kumbi or Ghana, Manding or Melle, Songhay, Bornu, Mossi, and Hausa. The records show that Ghana was in existence at least fifteen hundred years ago.

Gunga Musa was the most outstanding ruler of Melle. During his reign, from 1307 to 1332, Melle reached its peak. He enlarged the empire in all directions until it included the territory later known as French West Africa.

Gunga Musa became known to the outside world when he went on a pilgrimage to Mecca. Mohammedanism had become popular among the royalty and the rich. The rulers from the Sudan and West Africa made pilgrimages to Mecca. They did this to show their wealth as much as their devotion to the religion.

Gunga Musa had a good government. He knew how to take care of his money. He collected taxes on minerals and goods that came into the country. He also knew how to administer justice. The people were prosperous, as they were engaged in both industry and trade. They exported gold, ivory, skins, and kola nuts. The army was well organized, with both an infantry and a cavalry. The men were armed with bows and arrows, swords, and spears. There were two divisions of the army, one in the North and one in the South. The cavalry acted as the eyes of the army.

Sonni Ali

The next great empire was the Songhay. About the

year 1000 A.D., the empire occupied a large area along the Niger River. Its capital was called Gao. Shortly afterwards, the Songhay extended to Timbuktu; there was one man who was responsible for the rise of the Songhay empire. His name was Sonni Ali. He was one of the greatest rulers to appear in Africa.

Sonni Ali, as a boy, had been taken prisoner by Gunga Musa. Gunga Musa had gone to Gao to receive the homage of the Songhay. On his return trip from Mecca Gunga Musa captured Sonni Ali along with some other young men. After he had grown up, Sonni Ali watched for every chance to escape. He made friends; he stored arms to defend himself in case of pursuit. His well-planned escape was successful. He reached the Songhay and organized the army. He defeated the Melle Army and made Songhay independent.

Under Sonni Ali, the Songhay began to expand in West Africa and the Sudan. He realized the importance of getting control of the Niger River. He conquered first one bank of the Niger and then the other. He was able to turn back attacks by his enemies and enlarge his empire.

Sonni Ali introduced something new in African warfare. He made use of boats to defend as well as conquer territory along the Niger River. Boats had been used in African wars; however, they had never been used to such an extent.

Sonni Ali incurred the displeasure of the Mohammedans. Because he was building an empire, he was too busy to respect the ambitions of the new faith. The religious people stirred up opposition to Sonni Ali, but he destroyed all opposition to his rule. The majority of the Africans had not become Mohammedans. Sonni Ali realized that a people divided by religion could never become strong. He destroyed every hostile stronghold, while schools and mosques favorable to him were protected.

Sonni Ali wanted to form a new kind of government. This was not easy to do, as the conquered people didn't always stay conquered. The king of Mossi attacked Massina in 1477 and Walata in 1480. This made Sonni Ali realize that he had to improve transportation between centers of his empire. He could help Walata more quickly if he connected Walata with Timbuktu. He began to dig a canal; however, he did not finish it. The Mossi again invaded his territory. He drove them back. But on the way, Sonni Ali was drowned.

Askia Muhammed

The next great ruler of Songhay was Askia Muhammed. He was both a ruler and organizer. Sonni Ali was a stern man, often thought of as cruel. He built the Songhay Empire and ruled from 1493 to 1529. Because he was a Mohammedan, he gave special favors to Mohammedan mosques and schools. He became acquainted with scholars like Merhili, the Moroccan reformer. In 1497, Askia made a pilgrimag to Mecca. There he met Soyati and other Muslim doctors.

The pilgrimage of Askia Muhammed was different from that of Gunga Musa of Melle two hundred years before. He had a smaller number of people with him, he took less gold, and, in addition to his military escort, he had scholars and teachers.

Askia Muhammed went to Mecca to learn how to reform his government. He wanted his people to have better manners. When he returned to the Songhay he reformed the markets and trading structure. He introduced laws of inheritance and laws for the suppression of immorality. He limited religious intolerance and persecution, and concerned himself with the study of science, anatomy, law, literature, and grammar.

Askia Muhammed extended the empire. Melle had fallen to the Songhay by the end of the fifteenth century. Near the end of his life, Askia Muhammed became blind. In 1529 he was dethroned by one of his own sons. A half century later, the empire was broken up by the Sultan of Morocco.

75

CHAPTER 6

Contact with
Asia and Europe

The Mohammedans

Every culture has its great men. Black Africa, like other cultures, had its outstanding leaders. So little is known about Africa below the Sahara before the 1500's that we must rely on the accounts given us by a few historians. We do know that Africans below the Sahara and the upper Sudan had well organized governments and a life of trade and agriculture before the Mohammedans penetrated their lands.

Ibn Battuta traveled a great deal from West Africa to India and China. He was born a Berber in 1304, and died in 1377. During his travels he made notes about everything he saw. A book was made from these notes. It has become famous because of the interesting stories about West and East Africa during the fourteenth century. It is still one of the best travel books ever published.

Ibn Battuta traveled to the country of Mali in the middle of the fourteenth century. He crossed the desert with a caravan to Walata. Then he traveled to the capital of Mali by way of the Niger River. He visited Kilira and found it a beautiful and well built city. This was in the land of the Zanj in East Africa. Kilira was an important city on the coast.

He also traveled through the country of Melle. He noted that it was a prosperous country. It had a good government and a system of laws and justice. Public funds were handled wisely. He traveled in Melle during the reign of Suleiman, who had become ruler after the death of Gunga Musa. Ibn Battuta also reported on the customs of the Western Sudan and the famous ruler Askia Muhammed. Both the Songhay and its rulers have won their places in history.

Parts of Europe and Asia were close to Africa, and Asiatic and European people came to North Africa. Some Africans found their way into Europe. North Africa and Spain had many contacts. Europeans went to North Africa by way of the Straits of Gibraltar, and Africans reached Europe the same way. The Berbers, who were a mixture of Black and Arab blood, took over Spain in 711. Cordova in Spain became the center of culture when other parts of Europe were passing through the dark ages. The Christians in Spain finally drove the Arabs out.

Asiatics went to the east coast of Africa. It is known that the Chinese had contacts with the Africans. People from India established trading posts on the east coast. These people wanted gold, precious stones, ivory, and skins. However, no lasting impression was made by the Chinese or the Indians.

The Mohammedans swept out of Arabia into North Africa. Egypt was conquered by them in 638 A.D. During the next century they were a strong influence in all of North Africa. They had great success in establishing their religion. Penetration into the nations below the Sahara was a different matter, because the desert formed a great obstacle. Finally, the Mohammedans crossed into West Africa and the Sudan. Mohammedanism was accepted slowly by the kingdoms of Ghana, Melle, and Songhay. Kings and other rulers and the rich of these nations accepted the religion for political reasons and for purposes of trade. Most of the Africans kept their tribal religious customs.

The Mohammedans carried on slave trade. At first, Africans were bought and used in war. The demand for slaves grew larger and larger. The Moham-

79

medans enslaved people from large districts of Africa. Some African states profited by this slave trade. Slaves were used both as laborers and as soldiers.

Blacks were accepted as equals by the Mohammedans. If a slave embraced the religion, he could enjoy the advantages of the education and culture which the religion offered. Even as a slave, a black Mohammedan was considered as a brother.

The Portuguese

During the fifteenth century, Prince Henry of Portugal sent out men to trade in gold and slaves. The Portuguese ships made many trips down the western coast of Africa. Prince Henry died in 1460, but others kept on exploring. They went as far as the equator in 1471, and they reached the Congo in 1484. Diago Cam went a thousand miles south of the equator. Bartholomew Diaz and Vasco daGama went around the Cape of Good Hope. After this, many Portuguese ships sailed around Africa to trade with India.

Portuguese sailors found gold on the African coast. This spot was called the Gold Coast. They got gold and ivory from the Gold Coast traders. After the explorations of Prince Henry, Portuguese ships brought seven or eight hundred slaves to Portugal every year. The Portuguese influence in Africa was very strong until 1637. Their power was finally broken by the Dutch in wars that ended in that year. The Portuguese were then driven south by the Arabs on the east coast. By 1700, they lost all their territory there except Mozambique. They were able only to keep Angola on the West Coast.

In the fourteenth century, Africa was still a puzzle to the Europeans. The African interior was still unknown. A large number of black men had gone from the Sudan to trade with European ports. In the fifteenth century, there were about three thousand black men in Venice. It was Prince Henry of Portugal who, in 1418, began the exploration of this vast continent, Africa.

Glossary

Page 7   **ascend**—to move gradually upward

9   **sphinx**—a creature represented with a lion's body and a hawk's, ram's, or man's head

9   **obelisk**—a four-sided stone, shaped at the top like a pyramid

9   **reputed**—believed to be

12   **tribute**—a payment by one ruler or nation to another

18   **comptroller**—a royal-household official who examines and supervises the spending of money

19   **Afno-Hausa**—seven states in the land now known as Nigeria

21   **artifacts**—objects from past times

24   **intrusion**—the act of wrongfully entering upon

26   **unobservant**—not given to notice

28   **millet**—a grain

30   **aspect**—appearance

34   **gourd**—a hard-rinded fruit of plants, often used for ornament or for vessels and utensils

GLOSSARY

Page 35 **manioc**—root used to make tapioca
38 **taro**—root of a plant used for food
38 **sorghum**—a cane-like grass having a sweet juice from which syrup is made
38 **milled**—ground, as corn
39 **ficus (tree)**—fig (tree)
42 **sickle**—instrument for cutting grain
45 **embankment**—bank to hold back water
47 **implement**—one that serves as a tool
55 **allotted**—given
64 **enforcement**—putting into effect
72 **kola nut**—nut from kola tree, used as a condiment
74 **incur**—to bring down upon oneself

84

Bibliography

BONTEMPS, A. *Story of the Negro*. New York: Alfred A. Knopf, 1964.

DAVIDSON, B. *The African Past.* New York: Grosset and Dunlap, 1967.

FRANKLIN, J. H. *From Slavery to Freedom*. Second edition. New York: Alfred A. Knopf, 1964.

GREIG, M. E. *How People Live in Africa*. Chicago: Benefic Press, 1963.

HANSBURY, W. L., AND JOHNSON, E. H. *Africa's Golden Past*, Part I. New York: Ebony Magazine, November, 1964.

LINTON, R. *The Tree of Culture*. New York: Alfred A. Knopf, 1956.

SILVERBERG, R. *Empires in the Dust*. Philadelphia: Chilton Books, 1963.

SUTTON, F. *Illustrated Book About Africa*. New York: Grosset and Dunlap, 1966.

WOODSON, C. G. *African Heroes and Heroines*. Washington, D.C.: The Associated Publishers, 1944.

WOODSON, C. G., and WESLEY, C. H. *The Negro in Our History*. Washington, D.C.: The Associated Publishers, 1962.